READING POWER

Mark McGwire
Record Breaker

Rob Kirkpatrick

The Rosen Publishing Group's
PowerKids Press ™
New York

1

For my mother, a great reading teacher.

Published in 2000 by The Rosen Publishing Group, Inc.
29 East 21st Street, New York, NY 10010

First Edition

Book design: Michael de Guzman

Photo Credits: pp. 5, 9 © Brian Bahr/Allsport; pp. 7, 19, 21 © Vincent Laforet/Allsport; p. 11 © Reuters/Tim Parker/Archive Photos; p. 13, 17 © Otto Greule/Allsport; pp. 15, 23 © Rob Tringali Jr./SportsChrome USA

Text Consultant: Linda J. Kirkpatrick, Reading Specialist/Reading Recovery Teacher

Kirkpatrick, Rob.
     Mark McGwire: record breaker / by Rob Kirkpatrick.
     p. cm. — (Reading power)
   Includes index.
    SUMMARY: Introduces the player for the St. Louis Cardinals who set the home run record in 1998.
    ISBN 0-8239-5535-4
    1. McGwire, Mark, 1963– Juvenile literature. 2. Baseball players—United States Biography Juvenile literature. [1. McGwire, Mark, 1963– 2. Baseball Players.] I. Title. II. Series.
     GV865.M396 K57 1999
     796.357'092—dc21
     [B]   99-15999
                                        CIP

Manufactured in the United States of America

Contents

Mark McGwire plays baseball.

5

Mark plays first base.

7

Mark loves to hit the ball.
He has a big swing.

Mark hits a lot of home runs. In 1998, he hit 70 home runs! That is a record.

11

Mark was on the A's. The A's play in Oakland. In 1989, he helped the A's win the World Series.

13

Mark plays for the Cardinals now. The Cardinals play in St. Louis.

People like to see Mark at the ballpark. They come to see him hit the ball in batting practice.

Mark's friend Sammy Sosa makes him smile. Sammy plays for the Chicago Cubs.

19

Mark is best friends with his son, Matthew. Matthew likes to see his father's games.

21

Mark likes to be with people at the ballpark.

Here are more books to read about Mark McGwire:

Mark McGwire
by Richard Brenner
William Morrow & Company (1999)

Mark McGwire: Home Run King
(Sports Achievers)
by Jeff Savage
Lerner Publications (1999)

To learn more about baseball, check out this Web site:

http://cnnsi.com/

Glossary

batting practice (BAT-ting PRAK-tis) Hitting balls before the game.

home runs (HOHM RUHNZ) When a batter hits the ball out of the park and gets to run around the bases.

record (REH-kurd) An amount that beats what everyone else has done.

World Series (WURLD SEER-ees) When the best two baseball teams play at the end of the year.

Index

Word Count: 125

Note to Librarians, Teachers, and Parents

If reading is a challenge, Reading Power is a solution! Reading Power is perfect for readers who want high-interest subject matter at an accessible reading level. These fact-filled, photo-illustrated books are designed for readers who want straightforward vocabulary, engaging topics, and a manageable reading experience. With clear picture/text correspondence, leveled Reading Power books put the reader in charge. Now readers have the power to get the information they want and the skills they need in a user-friendly format.